A DOG IN
THE PARK

A DOG IN THE PARK

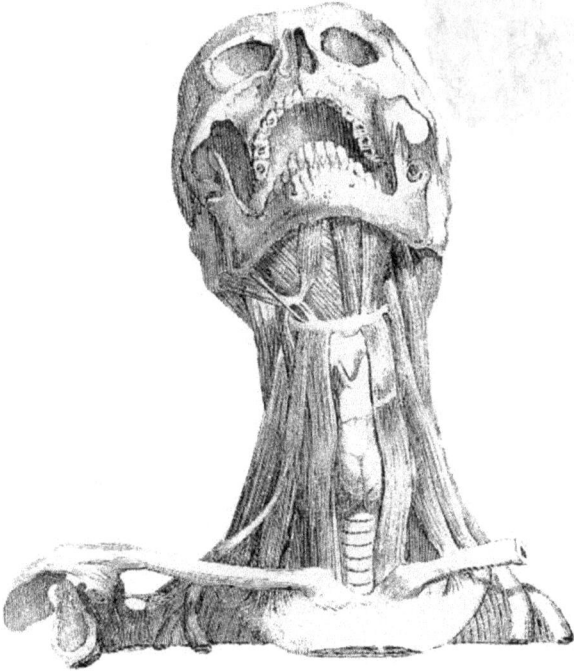

Geoffrey Mark Matthews

2015

First published 2015 by
PERENNISPEREGRINATOR

A Dog in the Park
©2015 Geoffrey Mark Matthews
photographs and cover design
©2015 Geoffrey Mark Matthews

ISBN 978-0-9932054-2-2

perennisperegrinator@gmail.com

A DOG IN THE PARK

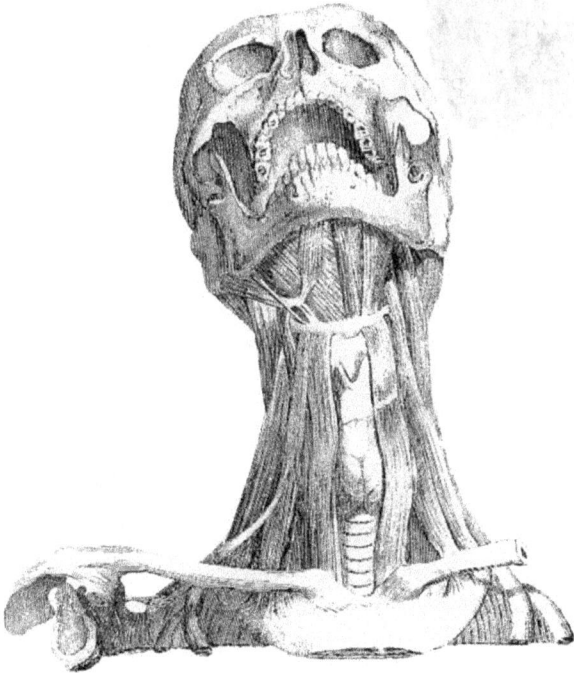

Geoffrey Mark Matthews

2015

First published 2015 by
PERENNISPEREGRINATOR

A Dog in the Park
©2015 Geoffrey Mark Matthews
photographs and cover design
©2015 Geoffrey Mark Matthews

ISBN 978-0-9932054-2-2

perennisperegrinator@gmail.com

Contents

It is in the Hobbesian state of nature that humans are 'wolves' to each other; but who turns the wolves into friendly, loyal dogs ?

Peter Sloterdijk, 'Rules for the Human Zoo.'

Quite an experience to live in fear, isn't it? That's what it is to be ... tame.

Ridley Scott (dir.), *Bladerunner.*

A DOG IN THE PARK

off leash in public
nosing drains
electric lines
gas leaks

you remember the purpose of money?

The dog is in a jar, or is it a bottle? Maybe it is in a box. The idea is to live on the street not in the road. People do it the world over. There are surreal comedy sketches set in perfectly furnished living rooms, except there is no room, just the furniture—sofa, armchairs, coffee table, TV, sideboard, fireside rug—and a family of four. And it is all on the street. You can't put furniture in the road and call it home. You would be between homes. The furniture would be packed up, tied down, covered with tarpaulin or polythene. It would be unusable. But on the street, where there is space enough between spaces, you can make it home if you need to or if you choose to. It isn't funny though. In the normal run of things you become invisible and miserable. Unless you are a dog, a fighting fit, totally barking, dog. But a dog does not need furniture. Any makeshift shelter will do. Any time of night or day, whenever you're tired, you just curl up inside the nearest empty container and sleep ... lightly.

Cursive hands

Hume famously had the look
of a turtle-eating alderman
Wittgenstein
of a waxen sheep-dipper
Foucault
of a piano molester and
Rorty
of a recently reupholstered
Queen Anne carver

and we wonder why
philosophers are listened to
so infrequently
so intensely
and to so little effect

periodically Socratic
they may be
but I say
thank them all for
writing and
dying in good time

The secret work-room

relying on sterner monsters
with something
of the edge to teach

dreams of mutation
distort reality
deviance enhances it

imagination feeds on
peripheral matters
seeking finality

life tests itself
through its freaks
becomes taut

Interrupting the Species[1]

a certain French artist
planned to deliver
to St. George's Hall
a hundred brightly painted oil drums
and thereby to
'interrupt the species'

such heroism

---

[1] Inspired by Christo and Jeanne-Claude: Wall of Oil
Barrels—The Iron Curtain (1961-62, Rue Visconti, Paris).

Imagination

far off and strong

enough to
manipulate mercury
jumble the seasons
dance with antiquity
and succumb
to true lies

this mental state
is the first misfortune

Confusion

earth shells
mineral fruits
insect stones

kings cast around
for relics of lust
while bundles bound in defiled skin
track the score

No virtue in extended fluidity

go on
patronize the reader
overload the poem with metaphor
make it too musical
because speaking is such a pleasure
extend the text
and seduce the eye by determining its shape

or accept that
the art is in accepting that
compressed substance emerges
regardless of your intentions

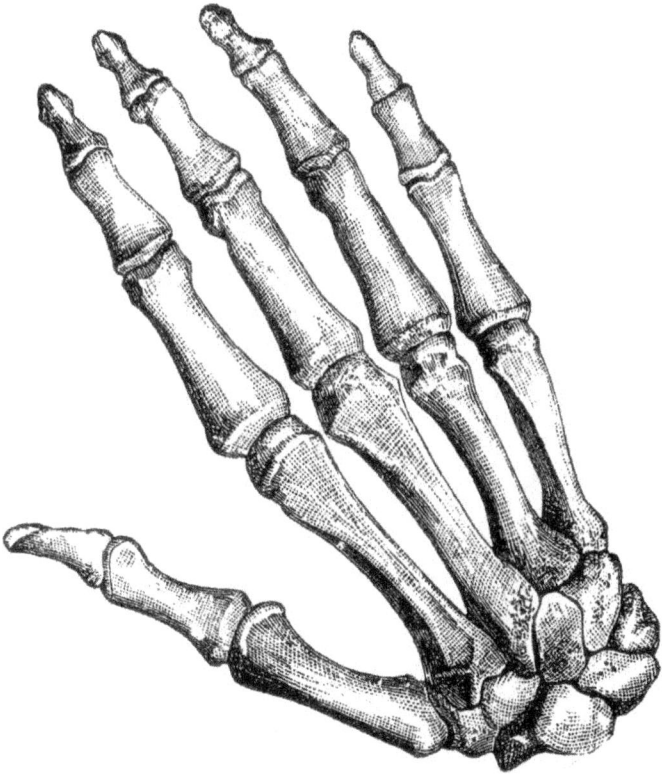

Party trick

the pope spoke of his hope
the king sang his gung ho song and
the soldier
soldiering on
shouldered the soul of an old colonialism
only to make a break
for the sake of sick mistakes
and risk swift redress
lead in the head
bled blood
good god
dead

Billy

how many times
   Billy Milligan died
   on his way to
   the cemetery
how many times
   he watched from afar
   the mourners gather
   graveside
   and smile
   wondering
how many times
   Billy Milligan died
David stands alone
   while Christopher
   blows blue notes on a harp
   and Adalana cries
Tommy dreams absently on
   while Danny recalls earthiness
   and Allen talks him out
Arthur and Ragen
   hold Christene's hands
   while warning off
   the undesirables
it's a solemn crowd
and
it's a solemn crowd
   beyond the wall
Samuel, Lee and Jason

April and Martin
Walter, Bobby and Shawn
Phil and Kevin
    all look in
Mark
    looks down
Timothy alone
    is oblivious
words spill
    from the teacher's brain
    willing Billy to appear
but here he is
    vanishing

Aqua vita

In memory of Carl Thorley

where is life?
not in the bones but in the sinews
singing from the swale of a favourite armchair
news from somewhere
some indelible somewhere

and when all the deliberate words have gone
one is left with the echoes
a swift river full of dissolved oxides
swirling around the house
arching over weirs and falls
slapping otherwise silent stone
notes from a dog-tired universe

an exemplary *vita activa*
drowned and drowned out
au revoir
dear friend

Place me

98 Eli Wallach
95 Richard Hoggart
93 Matilde Pérez
93 Manitas de Plata
91 Dannie Abse
90 Richard Attenborough
90 Frank Atkinson
89 Lauren Bacall
88 Tony Benn
85 Acker Bilk
82 Stuart Hall
82 Billie Whitelaw
80 Douglas Davis
80 Hans Hollein
76 Rodney Fitch
75 Sir Richard MacCormac
74 H. R. Giger
72 Alvin Stardust
71 Alistair McAlpine
71 Bob Hoskins
71 Jack Bruce
70 Colin Pillinger
70 Roy Bhaskar
68 Ranulph Glanville
63 Robin Williams
61 Jim Richard Wilson
56 Rik Mayall
46 Philip Seymour Hoffman

Atmospheres

fish frying fat
damp cobblestones
vegetable air
cigarette piss
winter and discontent

do we mourn the
young boy's loss
of innocence?
rail against the
intense hypocrisy that
characterizes our beloved
Britishness?

40 years on
all too aware now
of the necessary illusions of
organized existence
what legitimate role remains
but that of go-between?

Fury

filthy net curtain
draped from a dead sky
sun etched silk
at the scullery window
guilty downpour gliding
in like a parachute

it's a dreadful day

we walked six miles
sat
and watched the show
from a high dry stone wall
and returned to a
window seat full of wine

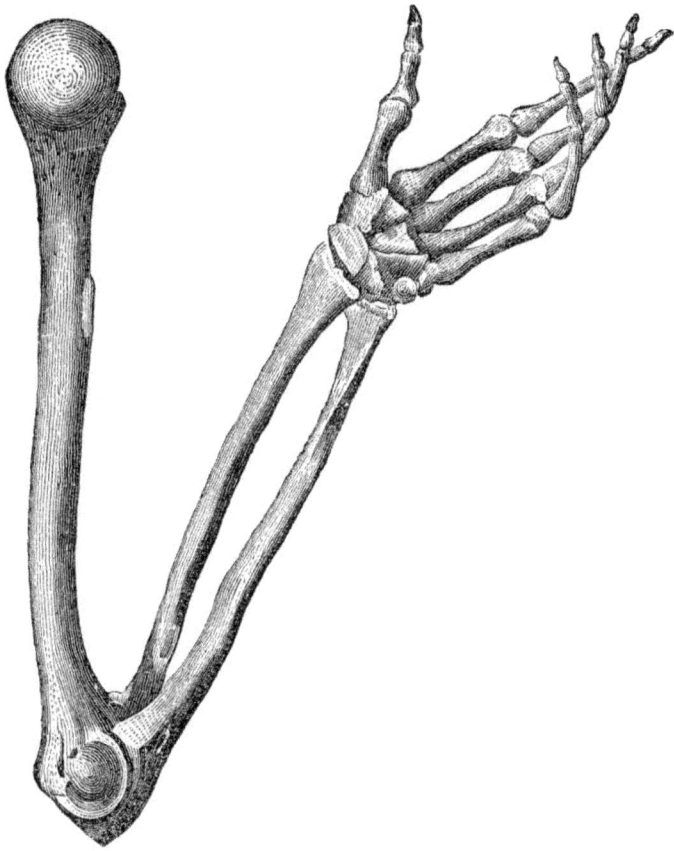

Denial

my distant son breathes machine air
skims a Martian sea for enriched faeces to eat
and dies alone
to face an unimagined
dies irae

more injured alien than progenitor
I ask the canon
in itself what is this human thing?
and unsatisfied
understand that even Icarus had
diasporic illusions

I know this
and still I grasp at paradise

The fabric of summer

shattered
   each spell an odyssey
think through the travails
abrupt storms that
   enmesh the head
mind silences of
   whining, humming and rushing
sultry squeezes
   bringing itchy sweat
   to every crevice
stenches
   drowning out mown grass
   and citrus zest
intermissions of
   movement in and out
indoor and outdoor haunts
   and tableaux annealed in sunlight
memory anodized to
   collide with rusty swarf
and its weight
   glassy and steely

Eclipse

it's an act
for which there is no measure

a perfect movement
loping
in an instant swooping
and then loping again

it takes a moment to realize
that the sun has dimmed
and brightened

Caustic reason

acoustic sticklers call for
Caucasian occasions licked clean of wit
and with what but a bit of
a boost in caustic reason?

The cat

the cat waddled backwards
the dollop of chilli con carne
only had to fall to the carpet
as it spewed forth

never seen a cat sick before
first time for everything

it's how they deliver gravel
in a tip-up trailer
edge it forward
gate open
bed raised

it slides out
like paste from a tube
paint off a Chinese brush
and that was the cat
the furry birthing mechanism
for a foot-long stain
on a brand-new Persian rug

Pasquinade

Caesar's
hair, nose and lips
disintegrate into
a lion's head

Asinius Pollio's
vast library
burning

Sloane remembers
mermaids wave as
giants drown

worn coin
scorched book
stained relic
all rendered august

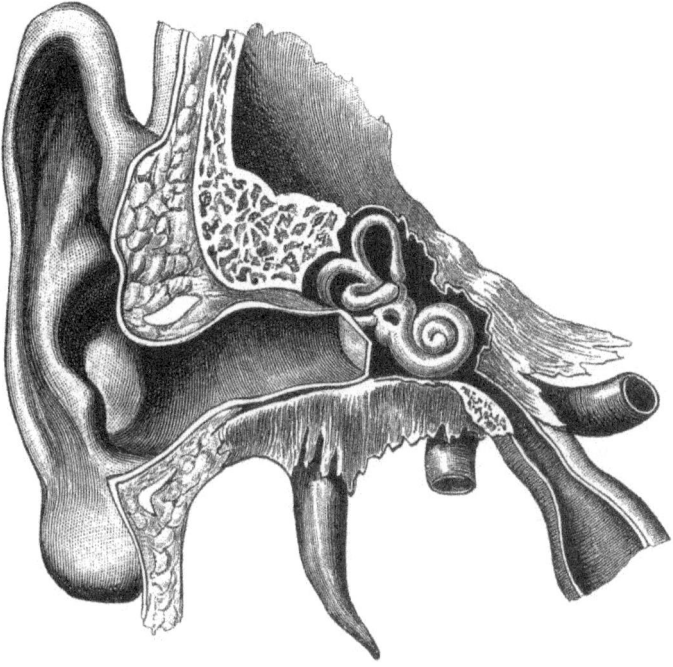

My mind drifted from a small incident in the present …

decaying cherry tom's replaced like
lying comrades withered in the soil
to which Albert, Stan and Charlie returned
year after year after year

that part of the salad relished
by sad men
whose energy drained
into entrenched patriotism

the sadness is
they also died

Albert had a trick he used
to distract the young lads
from their falling flesh
he drew this infinite regress of bell tents
disappearing in a line
drew the shrinking significance
of the cover
provided for ten men
when
within days
one might succumb to fever
another take a stray bullet
and so on
until so few remained

aromatic leaves
spring onions
finely chopped capsicum
and a drizzle of disease
so graves pass for positions
in eternity

Ruins of pleasure[2]

100

disappear
ruined Babylon
above the works of history

indeed
suspect that those stones
on buffalo carts
are seized by the country

cautious and secretive
they covered a space
to thrill the imagination and
caress desolation

time is inaccurate
a singular beauty
the strongest that particular words
can hardly express

200

pilgrims should be studied
and woven over by morals

---

[2] Source: Macaulay, *Pleasure of Ruins.*

the classic traveller
at the arena
is himself a ruin

still more unsteady
lament sometimes
only the confused fragments
of a vehement desire
in autobiography

the ripe rich greatness of the fallen
from a heap
a silent heap
filled with inscriptions

300

walls and broken apses
bathe noisily in the sea
and the sun
bleaches raiders

the enterprising
turned to a macabre pleasure
rampaging through spacious *triclinia*

foreigners painted
that much stupidity
clumsiness and greed

on walls of deep red

entertaining the famous
was a great art
already haunting the remains
in twenty glorious rooms

400

shattered walls all over
a closing vista
soothing and tranquil
foundations
reminding us of
the carved stone beams
before the earth quakes

their exploration was a quest
the most prodigious that has been
magnificent boasts
founded in the forest landing-place

coda

age
fragmented and fearful
climbs the dark crags
where the despots reigned on Greek hills
certainly nothing like Macao

and in the end their
... civilities
and deserts of time
treat ruins as toys
perhaps it is for the best

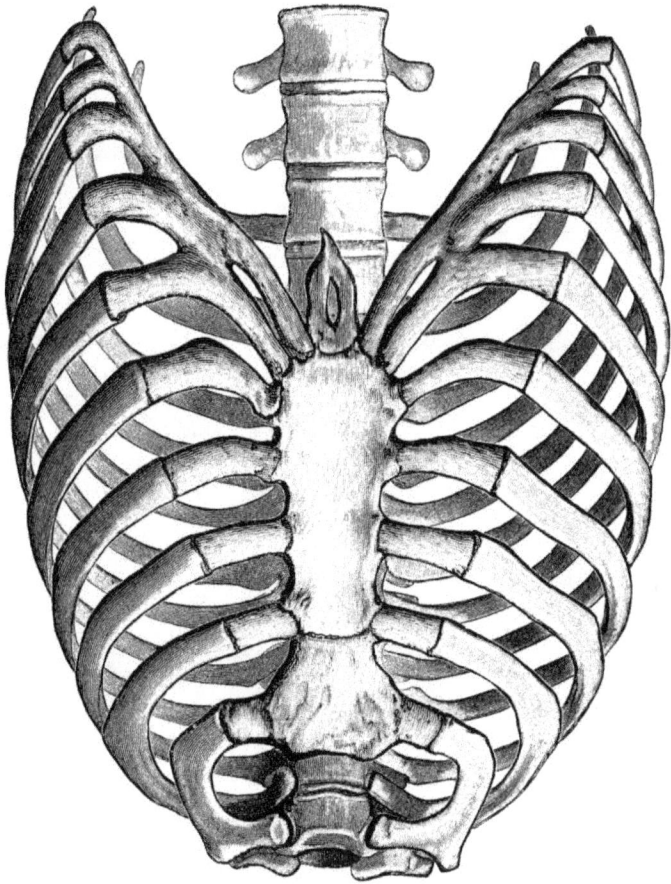

Big con rant

I have never understood why just because someone handles lots of other people's money they should be paid lots of money handling money is not an inherently difficult activity although those that do handle lots of other peoples' money have over the centuries deliberately mystified the activity and made it seem complicated just to convince people that they are doing something they could not possibly do for themselves and therefore convince them that they should be paid a lot of money for doing such a vital job even if they very often do not do a very good job but actually make a mess of it by getting so mixed up with the complexity of it all that they end up making mistakes and instead of making all that money turn into even more money make it into slightly less money or and sometimes this happens turning all of that money into a vast debt yes instead of handling the money and making it multiply handling the money and making it disappear making all the money that these people called clients owned disappear and a lot of money these people called clients never owned but that they borrowed on their behalf also disappear making these people called clients bankrupt and not bankrupt in some minor way but massively bankrupt and through all of this not a penny of the money they handled was ever theirs and yet they made sure that every step of the way to their clients' bankruptcy they were paid and paid handsomely paid huge sums of cash that they quietly stashed away in places where it could never be touched by anyone unqualified to handle it and of course there is only one person in the world qualified to handle their money … so you can probably understand why I think economics is just one enormous con it is far less real than the worlds of science fantasy and far more seductive far far more seductively seductive … and I have shit on my hands.

Posted on 31 May 2015:
https://perennisperegrinator.wordpress.com/2015/05/31/big-con-rant/

Front line report

I have just seen the Dog. I don't think he saw me, but he seemed to speak. This is what he said, I think: *Call off the gods. We are in this together and I know you know what needs to be done.* It was a mess. The microphone slipped out of my hand to be replaced by a gun. *This is America* I told myself. It may have been a Saturday afternoon in Doncaster market, but that's where my head was. Great!

The Dog, by the way, is a born leader; and the gods? They generally go around in a pack. Strange world, eh?

Posted on 31 May 2015:
https://perennisperegrinator.wordpress.com/2015/05/31/front-line-report/

The true meaning of anarchy

Vagrant porridge-brain is rapping at the front door, his tool-dog surveying the back. No chance now. Could've pelted down the ten-foot, wired the Volvo and been half way to Hell, but I missed it. Bollocks! They collect, these beggars: 'bailiffs of the conscience', I call 'em. *Thousands die every day. Where there's conflict, we're first in, last out. We save lives.* Who's this 'we', you nervy little geek? You've got the jacket, got the badge: doesn't make you a player though, does it? Out in the field? What fucking field have you been in? One filled with sheep and cows maybe? Your baby-arse face certainly never felt a bullet fly. Your hands were never washed in bystander blood. Not that I want you real. For fuck's sake, may as well twitter with the back-benchers of Warminster, you know, smug bastards revelling in the gullibility of idiots. It's all mock faith and violence by proxy. Give it a rest. I make choices: what to listen to, what to hear, when to speak, what to say. You want action? Watch me. You want my money? Want to infect me with guilt? Fuck off. FUCK OFF. ...

Posted 31 May 2015:

https://perennisperegrinator.wordpress.com/2015/05/31/the-true-meaning-of-anarchy/

We may yet saturate the earth with blood

Until ten thousand years ago wherever humans lived there was always somewhere else they could go to continue their endless movement into uninhabited land. Then things changed; all the habitable space had been colonized. History starts when encounter becomes certain, when the compression of human space begins, when conflict becomes unavoidable. History is the record of such interference.

Interference patterns normally shift continuously; sometimes they are constructive, sometimes destructive, but from time to time, a pattern momentarily stabilizes. Without reason or perhaps through sheer force, a civilization spreads over the land and things appear to take some larger shape. Space becomes more densely populated, strangely ordered and relatively, if only temporarily, stable: for nothing lasts.

Civilizations are mere blips in an otherwise unstoppable human lust for dominion. We may yet saturate the earth with blood.

Posted on 27 May 2015:
https://perennisperegrinator.wordpress.com/2015/05/27/we-may-yet-saturate-the-earth-with-blood/

Lost in space: exiled on earth

The two cities of my middle life could be contrasted thus.

The first was cast in the form of an ever-diminishing triangle, disorientating, introverted and without elevation. Its circuit of docks lay broken, land-filled or land-locked, for the days of journeying in from the lagoons, forests and moors, and out to the seaboards of the world were over, but for one dreaded ferry and one infernal bridge to nowhere. The city sat on the north bank of a great estuary into which flowed the river that divided it, identified it, and called its time.

The second was thrown like a seed from some long distant past and grew axial. It rose from marsh to ridge, or sank from bastion to basin according to which way one faced: to the pole star or to the sun. Always one is clear about one's place; however one proceeds there is that geodesic inscribed in the earth, from which one deviates only to be drawn to return. At one end is heaven at the other hell; in between stories of domesticity, commerce, trade, burial, agriculture and adventure unfold in descending order.

Like Calvino, I am hidden, like de Quincey, adrift. Both cities have preposterous pasts, ingrained in memory as a boy and as a young man. Living in them, later in life, involved the elaboration and distortion of their myths rather than their demythologization. In this regard I am not a Modern and not an Ancient. I am older still, a sedentary nomad, an immortal troglodyte, like Robinson, lost in space, like Borges, exiled on earth. And how do I become this way? The barbarians have been and gone, transformed into a coalition of mutually repulsive powers, a constellation of force fields. Matter and energy are one in the politics of vanity, in the molecular cosmos. And the dissident, the maverick, the rogue electron, each finds many resting points on its abounding peripheries.

Posted on 31 May 2015:
https://perennisperegrinator.wordpress.com/2015/05/31/lost-in-space-exiled-on-earth/

The difference between a dream

The front step turned blue. It was dead. The light shone sideways and the step was dead. Nothing would retrieve its delicate blush at this late hour. I saw a single hair. It was stuck to a blemish: some terrible infant's careless graze. This we could blame for the rise of such a colour, such a blue.

Our witness remained outside. He saw the eyes, but not the hair that I had seen. The scene became drenched in pathetic money; for a hair, ten dollars, for a second glance, many, many golden sovereigns. They rise up like neon filled sausages, blaring their insoluble symphonies through the grey mud of nightfall. They hammer the temples and sever the optics, shattering them into sea spray: it portends a *neuromancy* of spectra. And what is yet to come? Yes, what is yet to come?

The front step turned blue, very, very blue. But I did not need to see it. I felt its cobalt radiance in the depths of the dream. It was dead, dead as the oldest death, the death of a reflex, but not as dead as silence. The light shone sideways, not because of any reflex, but because all else was extinguished.

The lake fell away taking love with it, reversing the onslaught of evolution and the blending of one unit with the mysterious circle of life. Copper, tin and various powdered minerals hide the bacteria of business. It clinks in deep pockets. It registers as dumb. It rules the sad gestures exploding from burdened minds. It brings on nerve exposure to ice deep within the bones of paranoia's playground.

Sleep me. Sleep me with your rainbow words. Take me one step lower, and another, and another. And let the first step enter the sky with grace to hide behind lowered eyelids and to hum with expectation. Horizon fruit blotches the living image and every blinking aversion. I am stabbed in the brain with a tuning fork. Spiders escape from my ears, millions of irritant crabs screaming on a pinhead. Look down, there is no choice but to look down, and see the complementary colour flood seamed with broken gold.

Posted on May 27, 2015:
https://perennisperegrinator.wordpress.com/2015/05/27/the-difference-between-a-dream/

Next

I hadn't felt this bad since Doug crashed out on May Day last year and brought down the biggest flood of exotic bugs in the history of my little fiefdom. Here I was coughing up green, some of it flecked with blood. Uugh! How do I even get my normally so universally disciplined mind to recall such stuff? So, I felt bad. The English were bowling out the Aussies in double quick time. You can't smell the crowd through the radio, at least you are not supposed to, even with powerful extension speakers. But I could smell something—popping Cane Toad, Fruit Bat guano, Crocodile breath—it hummed of pure antipodean disgust. So why did I feel bad? The English were bowling out the Aussies in double quick time, and I am English! You needed to be there to understand.

Posted 31 May 2015:
https://perennisperegrinator.wordpress.com/2015/05/31/next/

Great Tits

In the matter of free food there is definitely a pecking order, a hierarchy of species. It is not easy to tell what this is, however, until one observes the behaviour of individuals and of flocks visiting the garden. Look where feeders have been hung from the lower branches of small trees. Size matters, although it is not always the larger birds that take precedence. Starlings are aggressive, it is true, and will soon see off a group of House Sparrows. But a flock of Great Tits will also push the Sparrows a short flight away, where they will cluster below a roof ridge or on a hedge top to wait for the opportunity to return to the seeds and nuts. These birds will compete with their own kind but not with others. The Great Tits will dart in and out to the feeder from neighbouring branches. They will make startling turns and land as suddenly as the first chip of hail on a summer lawn. Never more than two birds will stay on the feeder at any one time. When a third arrives it will be challenged and will need to respond to stand any chance of feeding.

Posted 31 May 2015:
https://perennisperegrinator.wordpress.com/2015/05/31/great-tits/

Over the border, living on

No-one dies anymore. People get killed of course—there are plenty of accidents, some suicides and the occasional homicide—but otherwise life goes on and on.

There are diseases—viral, bacterial, the full panoply—but they have become … mmm … theoretical, curiosities, play things for the biologically minded. All of them have been tamed, contained, objectified, bottled and catalogued, ready to amuse and to edify. Like everything out of scale with human conviviality they now have their security enclosure and their surveillance machinery. And this universal heritage makes money in its idleness through the devotion of spectators. It has become an industry. There are great repositories for all the sad, bad, redundant and external things of the world, all the stuff that we do not need or, more correctly, all the stuff that does not need us any longer. There are laboratories and workshops and theatres and galleries where people study them endlessly and archive their reports. There are people who bury themselves in the mountains of words to open up painted caves echoing with the ritual of discourse. They think and write and talk, and rethink and rewrite and talk again. In this way the stories emerge that keep us sane and together—humans need habitable chambers. But there is a problem with this, one last problem that no-one so far has been able to solve. A chamber too easily becomes a prison that freezes one's insides, and this is worse than the death of which one can now only dream.

Everyone needs a bit of excitement from time to time, and everyone needs some down time as well as opportunities for raw experience, recuperation and reflection. Emotional variety, you see: without it we make no memories, existence lacks structure, and life has no meaning. In reality life does not have any meaning, of course: it is an illusion, a necessary illusion. I mean, we are talking about how the mind works not the whole world. The point is: there is a fine line between a healthy emotional life and the kind of psychological instability that can take a person down and it is a very individual thing. What is good for you might be disastrous for me and vice versa, and what is worse, getting older makes space for more and more disasters.

The danger period interestingly is the ten years around the age of one-hundred-and-fifteen—what used to be regarded as the natural terminal age for humans. The days merge into shrinking weeks. Seasons tumble in a visible rhythm conjuring up a fear of inevitabilities. As one passes into a living afterlife, so to speak, it may start to feel like being a slave. One may be so jaded that one starts looking for a way to break the rhythm.

Although I am way past this danger point, yesterday I contacted a friend who shares my curiosity concerning mortality's horizons. Our conversation is a strangely calm one, one becoming of philosophers or therapists locked in mutual forensic dissection. And we land on the question of *visiting Rome*. We wonder when in life it is an appropriate undertaking, and whether one should unburden oneself first and enter 'naked' or one should carry a wealth of ornaments, muniments and armaments into the mêlée.

We agree that the time is right for us to turn to the Eternal City for no other reason than the persistence of the image in our deliberations. Regarding the correct approach, however, we are less certain. One cannot rely on received wisdom as a guide for there is none, and formal histories are not much help either. Custom is, as far as one can tell, an entirely local and occult matter. For example, intoxications derive from many different poisons, which are available according to tradition and scarcity as often as to fashion and commerce, and the whole business of pushing the limits of indulgence is not something openly discussed anymore. My friend and I know the myths—Juan Matus's jimsonweed, William Lee's bug powder, De Quincey's "enthralment," Huxley's mescaline, Hunter S's excesses, etcetera—but neither of us is aware of all the possibilities; how could we be? And, in any case, what interests us is something other than exploring the mind's malleability to stimulate creative production. It is not the exotic reaches of the landscape we wish to visit but its lost border.

I take the ego-diminished view that whatever the body wishes to express deserves respect because such communication precedes and gives rise to reason. I believe, therefore, that it should not be artificially restrained. My friend and I agree on this point. We have decided, therefore, that the naked approach is the one more consistent with our desperate hunger. It challenges propriety, to put it mildly. Nevertheless, we will risk full flight and raw encounter and see what happens.

We arrange for a monumental inscription on broken Carrara marble:

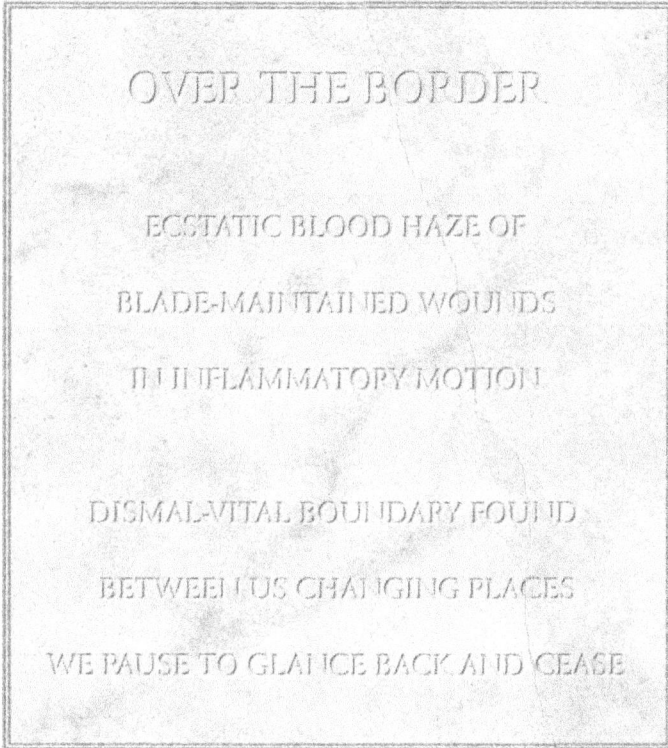

OVER THE BORDER

ECSTATIC BLOOD HAZE OF

BLADE-MAINTAINED WOUNDS

IN INFLAMMATORY MOTION

DISMAL-VITAL BOUNDARY FOUND

BETWEEN US CHANGING PLACES

WE PAUSE TO GLANCE BACK AND CEASE

Posted 22 February 2015:
https://perennisperegrinator.wordpress.com/2015/02/22/over-the-border-living-on/

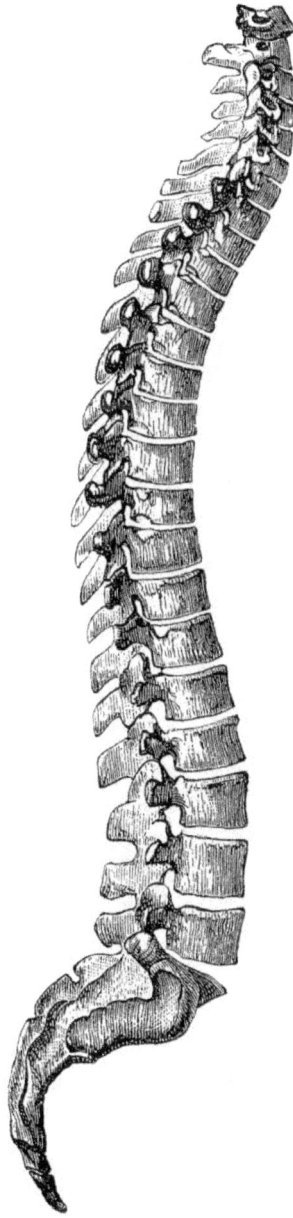

Activity or despair[3]

by himself entire
    he travels still
    fecund and knowing
his experience is a taking place
    though the whole has vanished
    and tradition as well
and his bodily exertion
    between four walls
    recedes into introspection of them

such a man is unreadable
    without the reality of a drift
    through the zoo city
speak further
    of a body social
    expanding into the world
where wealth is
    the mutually inclusive
    excellence of human parks

one canon
    in this world of unhindered bodies
    can forgive us non-sovereignty
dignity is a caricature

---

[3] Sources: *The Human Condition* by Hannah Arendt, *Wanderlust* by Rebecca Solnit, and *The Aesthetics of Disappearance* by Paul Virilio.

of being a bloody canyon
in the landscape
call the land
scars and spoils
task the wild woodsman

in a dark age
make imaginary landscapes
and dream of earth
block-in artifice and dreaming
as an arrival
and its consummation
so all the years of building
diminish the man
and the past agrees

it starts in light
in the north
of the world
in the intensity
of rarer terrains
and cultures
in both
fascinated children are
... delivered

Liquid

the liquid in the bottle felt
monastic and magnetic
it swam with pleasures
of a tortuous kind
like failing jokes and
freshly re-swept floors

set black in the acids
of rolling decades
in vitro ruminations
follow on

from puce dribbles
and craquelure
scattered monoxide lines
on yellowed paper
form memory fragments
of alien mammals'
forgetfulnesses
and thoughtlessnesses

they too are a cynic's pleasures
we do not use them though
they must not
be allowed to fly
or be smeared
on further parched surfaces
they must forever swim

the amoebic
draught of *aqua*
hitting its *vita*

Naked return[4]

cramps of loneliness
minimal efficacy
reversed nightmare forgetfulness
scream in silence
shielded thicket lit by fear
corneal seas slowly confound expectation
perverted phantom whores

---

[4]   Matthews, *from Moving Window to Cave*, p. 69-70

Gimping

you're a fantasy
I want you to
drink a bottle of whisky a day
smoke fat cigars
and die
before I do

Intrusion

the letter-plate bang
strikes me blank
in the bones

the phone rings
and I sink down
in my fear

...

Fragile

visions
soluble in dream
dive back into
cavern mother

I ride the vortex
otherwise extended
taut brittle
in a sliver of stench

my shoulder shudder
warns of thieves in the whirlwind
of the Narcissus saltie
poised to snap if I shatter

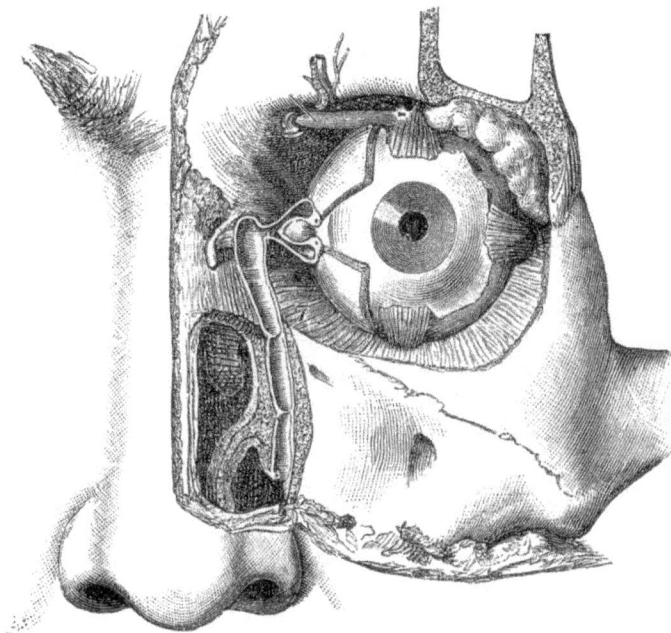

Mourning the With

the gritters have gritted
teeth shatter

the Ego must breathe
though insulated from
the dark
the anarchic thoughts
of the With
that withers after birth

never at home
either of us

What the fuck Said

he starts in the heart
of overlapping territories
    somewhere to confuse
    the barbarian
    even as he takes
    his pleasure

Calypso's concealment and compliance
    something to resist
    through movement
    without travelling

the Cyclopes' rabid consumption
    something to escape
    through migration

the cycle begins again
    with grasping amnesia

Al-Farabi's Altamira[5]

into earth

Maria walks through porous walls
where fleeting spirits swarm
as frozen shadows

she feels the thirst and hunger
of ancestors chasing
animals back to life

she sinks to save
the invisible city
from barbarism

she escapes the cave
reclaims the world
for nomadism and

she descends again
to dwell

---

[5] It was Maria, daughter of amateur archeologist Marcelino
Sanz de Sautuloa, who wandered off alone and discovered
the prehistoric wall paintings in the Altamira cave in 1879.

About what?

Gene said
a song can be about anything[6]
maybe your stubbed toe
or the Russian recession
or candyfloss
or the dustbins filling with shit
or the last Colorado Beetle in Colorado
or his mother died and her father lied
or a crack in bridge 002B
it's all the same to me

but it is not so
a song can only be about
being

being held in thrall to
the great myth
of unity
one world!
one thought! [7]

and what if it falls?
splits the split atom
and lands beyond beyond
what about that?

---

6   Genesis P-Orridge, the Prism Archive, part 5.
7   Sloterdijk, Intense Idyll, p. 24.

two-and-a-half thousand years
of circling back to the beginning
where a little voice says
do not pass go
but we pass go
to circle again
and again

and what about *this* time?
this *time*, ha!
this time
we arrive at
God is a big bang
the biggest bang ever
an originary big bang
so
do not pass go
there is nowhere left to go
then
bugger me if we don't pass go
and circle again

oscillating multiverses Batman!
quiet Robin
you don't get to perpetuate the myth that easily

back to the ~~Bat~~ Cave

to Swale

this gouged-out channel of darkness
loops hesitant dullness
uncertain of the turbulence
deep in the cold-fish pool
beneath the new bridge

it swirls black between white-water shallows
one breaking for the keep
the other for the kirk
unholy and holy in a sacred clinch
of Akkadian origin

with orderly tensions
this affliction bridges
the stone-face fixity
of living

uncomprehending barbarian kings and clansmen
still cling to deceit
    and bigotry
    and ignorance
    and hypocrisy
still sow seeds in anaerobic slime
and wonder why they rot

and haunting me
so stands the hallowed and swaled town
riddled with its charcoal beasts

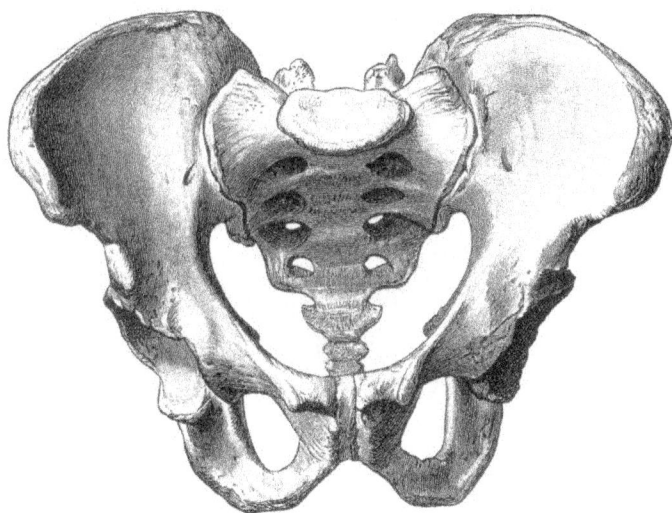

Distant voices

in the heart of the bubble
delusional lizards
suffocate on red hot rocks
believing they have dominion

this pool of distraction
is called
the people

Teaching and learning

I can't see for the stinging rain of wasted words
crusted oratory on the bottom of a bathmat
colonies of woodlice creeping into the minds of wistful
                                                    listeners
hives of busy wives and house husbands
maternally yours and mine
and blind to the smouldering matter
pitched between the politician's greed
and the teacher's plea for freedom
the guarantee we seek sits in the creases of burning
                                                    foreheads
not on sweaty benches or in the semen-stained and
power-pained seats of limousines
dream on, dream on, dream on

complicit in their own containment professors profess
stiffly murmuring soft words of reassurance that graze
                                                    and irritate
not sterile and anaesthetic but positively poisonous
like perfect columns of toothpaste
drawn across backyard bristles
to make our gums bleed and leave the teeth
                                                    contaminated
what's needed is a caustic rant on the myth of American
                                                    teeth
(Tony, where is it?)
a nuclear blast to expose all the Eastern teeth that hide
                                                    behind raised hands

a winding engine to pull all the hollow teeth rooted in
                                    the European lie
dream on, dream on, dream on

sat fat-arsed and glued to the plush velvet
drunk on sycophantic drooling and talking in wet-farts
well-meaning veterans decay into corruption
I can't hear any more for the blinding light that shines
                                    overhead
the roar of the lions as they leave their den
and every night the shipping forecast
that casts the land lubber into that beautifully false
                        feeling of suspended animation
those in peril are here not out on the waves and waving
                                    good bye
leaving the lions to surround us in the heat of debate
and when we least expect it drown us in hate and clamp
                            irons around our heads
dream on, dream on, dream on

I can't see and I can't hear any more
I can smell something though
and I can feel it
it tastes of hope

The smell of the sea

the smell of the sea
    you can taste
    and drown
no word seethes
    more than
    seaweed
forget
    brown, red and green
    the deep is gold

so forlorn
    ogres sip and thirst
    near grand banks
with the fish
    old crabs
    spiral and foam
clawing for flesh
    and surfacing for
    cesspit respiration

Collapse

the days went by
there was nothing to it
prehistory repeating itself? Not quite
but there is a recognizable pattern.

we could never know the
precise topology that was forming
as it approached in a
tumble of chaotic operations

the oldest ice did not
straightforwardly
absorb heat from the sun
and melt

it was an occult inducement
to catastrophe
tickled from below and enticed
to slide ever more quickly
into the deep turbulence but
this was neither cause nor effect
in the collapse

a dominant species
never remains dominant
for long

Shirase's prayer[8]

no escaping
the howlers that allowed
escape from breaking floes
heart break
forms a black threshold
between lycanthropic poles

an abysmal sphere enthrals

fearing each side of night
Shirase sips the Buddha's cup
a *banzai* of regret
that burns away sorrow
and secret desire
all too slowly

---

8 Shackleton could "burn with a strange passion for the
   South" but as for Shirase, no-one could match the man's
   sorrow.

   Hamblyn, 'Wilderness with a cast of thousands.'

Odourless

orcas circle and
in seconds take
a solitary seal
from cracked ice

vultures circle and
land for an hour to
skeletonize a corpse
on cracked earth

across the reach
lavender hangings at the windows
scent the noisome laws
escaping with the lies and laughter

Garden

in the low light
leaves knife the wind
fine twigs stab the sky
and the fences blaze russet

Pied Wagtail
Song Thrush and Coal Tit
occulted and clashing
Blackbird
Robin and Goldfinch
perfect in colour and counterpoint

gorse and bramble
sycamore seedlings
ivy-strangled lilac
and too-tall firethorn

strimmer whining through meadow
secateurs chopping whippy stems
livid wheals on arms and legs
blistered fingers in heavy canvas
compacting the wheelie-bin

reluctant war
perfect and perilous therapy

At a stroke
(for Dick McConnell)

the persistence of a Blue Whale's moan
may shatter the smoothest stone on the shore
and it doesn't matter who looks on

the spirit sings to the ones who listen
to the waves
to the warnings
and rise from the beach still smiling

Inland

perfect white teeth
clenched to bite back
remind the screaming black head
of its aching for the shoreline

soaring on icy stillness
above the seething
the night continues
in a waking dream

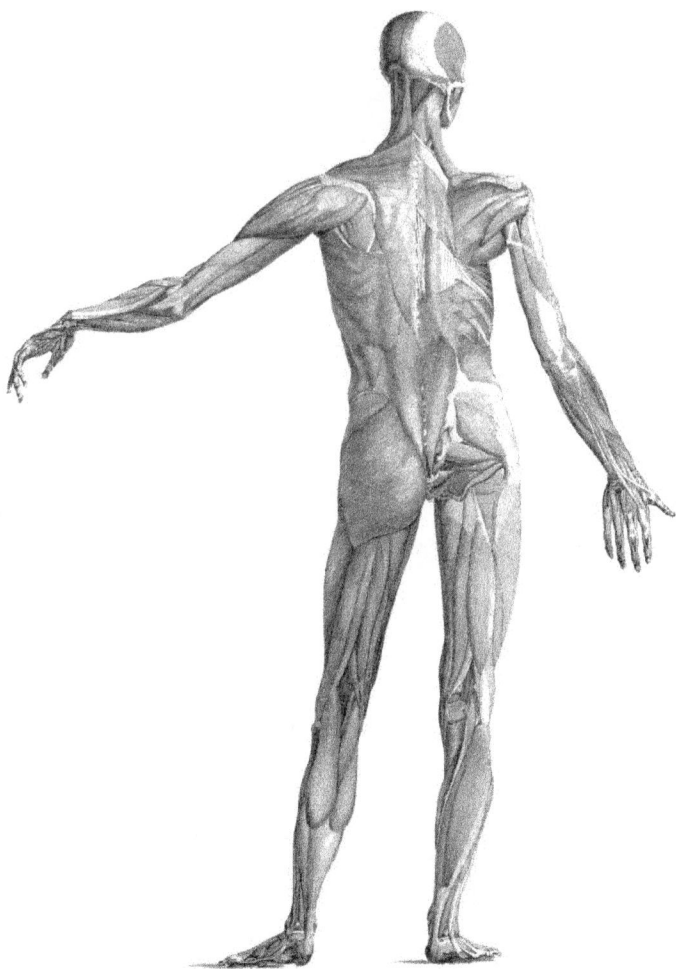

Modern cynics[9]

conceited silk and apathetic fat
luxuriating in purple and linen
snarl and bark

inhumane
narcissistic and greedy
fuelled by disdain and
dismissive of the living

you may be
educated, positioned and polished
Your Lordship
Your Grace
Your Majesty
but you have nothing of
Diogenes heart and bite

I shit on your heads

---

[9] Source: Modern Cynicism.

Fear

a dog wanders through wooded edges
intoxicated by the presence
of absent enemies
cocking a leg and pissing
on one bit of bark after another
adding to the legislation
discourse
and commerce of odour

the strong taint the litter
runts rise
to hunt and be hunted
in the dark
and the world dies a little

terror ends in memory's empty halls
until the nose takes over
and we smell the morning
to which order and submission belong

it is easy to insist on indifference
simply inhale

Canine thought

whether lost or cast adrift in a white sky
the centre explodes
slowly
so
at best
a mental murmur remains

a ballooning boredom of broken vapour
set wandering aloft
bellows
in an arc
goes east and west
is beset with mesmerising wishes

easier than peaks and pebbles
soft woods weather
peeling
crumbling
birch and ash
deliver creaks of dreams

bones glow with fleeting wisdom
grip the crook and
ache
dip
and graze the path
with ferocious sight lines of memory

watch with silent breath and listen
listen out of politeness
shh
there
an irresistible call
wresting a distant king from oblivion

Prospects of ubiquity

isn't it time to explore
   heads-up
   eyes-down
   minds-eye
the sources of independence?
not how?
but why?
couples under cover
   delicately dedicated
   to nomad myth
enrich the torch-lit circle
   with passion's favourite eye
dispense mystery
   routinely to the stars
even the dimmed
   and the vanished
we trust
   such dubious symbols of paradox
as a way of
   entertaining the past and
   entering the territory
hounds move in line
   and then fan out
savage layers
   simply uttering the words
   makes them salivate
they leave after dusk
   inferences of

bites and burnt states
for the lost to find
each
a resilient exception to
outsider map-maker laws

Mad not insane

people still crawl
to media demigods but
even with a grip on mammon
they cannot save him

blank and outcast
ghosting streets
and backyards
for a desert haunt
dog-like
he raises an engulfing rage

Stomach

I turned three times curled up and suffered
it was the feasting at night
the running through streets to celebrate
and the returning too late to know
that bandits were outside the walls again
that's what did for me

they drummed and chanted and made camp
settling in for a siege
all the while lifting dry stones from the fold
scattering material then
beating me down in my restless dreams
to knot the gut

no matter how prolific reason may be
how secure its treasury
cunts like these can dissolve it all in bile
and disable the love
it is as well that I am strong enough to resist
uncurl and vomit fresh deposits

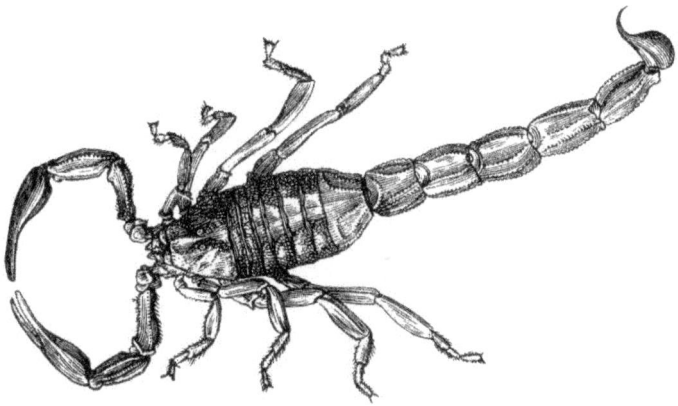

References

———— 'Modern Cynicism,' *Blackwood's Edinburgh Magazine*, January 1868, vol. 103, no. 627, pp. 62-70. <http://babel.hathitrust.org/cgi/pt?id=uc1.32106019932 133;view=1up;seq=70> accessed 24-05-2015.

Arendt, Hannah. *The Human Condition*, (1958, Chicago: University of Chicago Press).

Genesis P-Orridge, the Prism Archive, part 5, 00.01.54-00.03.20. https://www.youtube.com/watch?v=mbLje8H_Qyg (accessed 31 May 2015)

Hamblyn, Richard. 'Wilderness with a cast of thousands,' *The Times Literary Supplement*, No. 5743, 26 April 2013, pp. 8-9.

Harter, J. (ed.) *Images of Medicine* (1991, New York: Bonanza Books).

Macaulay, R. *Pleasure of Ruins* (1953, London: Weidenfeld and Nicolson).

Matthews, Geoffrey Mark. *from Moving Window to Cave* (2015, Lincoln: Perennisperegrinator).

Scott, Ridley (dir.) *Bladerunner*, (screenplay: Hampton Fancher & David Peoples), 1982.

Sloterdijk, Peter. 'Intense Idyll' in *Globes: Spheres II* (2014: South Pasadena: Semiotext(e)), pp. 13-43.

Sloterdijk, Peter. 'Rules for the Human Zoo,' *Environment and Planning D: Society and Space*, 2009, volume 27, pp. 12-28.

Solnit, Rebecca. *Wanderlust: A History of Walking* (2000, New York: Viking Penguin).

Virilio, Paul. *The Aesthetics of Disappearance* (1991, New York: Semiotext(e)/Autonomedia).

Colophon

Where indicated earlier versions of the prose pieces first appeared on the perennisperegrinator blog as did the poem 'Aqua vita.' All other poems are published here for the first time. I have neither sought nor received any financial assistance towards the writing. I did my own photography and page layouts, and the illustrations are adapted from copyright-free engravings in Harter, *Images of Medicine*. As the quotes I have used are very short, no specific copyright clearances have been sought.

Geoffrey Mark Matthews is an artist and writer and lives in Lincolnshire. He was born in 1954 and grew up in North Yorkshire. His other collections of poems are, *pausing at Anger* (1985), *The Familiar Reaches* (2004 and 2015), *Dead Reckoning* (2009) and *from Moving Window to Cave* (2015).

notes

notes

www.ingramcontent.com/pod-product-compliance
Lightning Source LLC
Chambersburg PA
CBHW071608040426
42452CB00008B/1283